I CAN OVERCOME MY FEAR,ANXIETY AND WORRY: SHUN OUT THE MONKEY MIND

John S. McCloud

Table of contents

CHAPTER 1 : **What is Fear?**

CHAPTER 2 : **Understanding your Anxieties**

CHAPTER 3 : **Understanding your Worry**

CHAPTER 4: **Stress Test – Part 1**

CHAPTER 5 : **Self-Inventory**

CHAPTER 6 :**Technique 1 : Mindfulness**

CHAPTER 7 : **Technique 2: Visualisation 1**

CHAPTER 8: **Helpful Tips**

CHAPTER 9: **When to See a Professional 1**

CHAPTER 10: **When to See a Professional 2**

CHAPTER 1

What is Fear?

Fear can be defined in a number of different ways. Each definition helps unlock specific clues that will help you to eventually conquer your fears.

As you go through each definition of fear, ask yourself whether it applies to your situation:

Irrational Beliefs
Fear is a set of erroneous ideas you have about objects, events or your actions. Your beliefs control what you focus on and pay attention to. These ideas also control your decisions and actions. As a result, your life is dominated by notions that probably don't have any validity in reality. They are irrational, or in other words, they are made-up beliefs that you utilise as a safety mechanism to protect you from potential suffering. The quicker you let go of these ideas and instead replace them with a set of rational empowering beliefs that are rooted in fact, the sooner you take back control over your worries.

Sense of Uncertainty
Fear is a sensation of uncertainty you have about future outcomes or conditions. You don't know what will happen next, and as a result, you fear whatever is hiding and waiting for you around the corner. In order to

progress past this, you need to gather relevant knowledge, information, and assistance that will help you to gain more clarity.

Uncertainty is nothing more than a lack of information or perspective you have about something. Simply find the information that is lacking, and your fear of uncertainty will likewise disappear.

Distorted Expectations

Fear is a collection of false expectations you have about future outcomes. Instead of using your imagination to construct a terrible future, use your imagination instead to think about all the wonderful consequences that may result from your activities. Quit giving yourself all these tales about what could go wrong, and instead get into the habit of telling yourself stories of how things might turn out in your favour.

Distorted Memories

Fear is a set of distorted memories you have of past experiences. You are essentially using your imagination to exaggerate past events in a way that promotes fear in the present moment. Choose instead to think about your memories differently – in a way that will help empower you rather than discourage you.

What is Fear and What are the Consequences

The Negative Consequences of Fear

Living in fear has only one main advantage: it keeps you very alert. However, there are no sabre-tooth tigers or mammoths hiding around the corner threatening your livelihood. It therefore absolutely makes no sense at all to live in fear during the 21st century. Fear will only stifle your motivation, prevent you from growing emotionally and from developing new skills that can help you to make progress in life.

Fear can also stifle your intellectual growth and will certainly lead to very poor decisions. In fact, the poorest and most irrational decisions are always made out of fear. These decisions often lead to unfavourable consequences that could have easily been avoided if you learned to overcome, or at least to better manage your fears.

Finally, fear often breeds destructive behaviour, resistance, and insecurity. It will literally rob you of your livelihood, and prevent you from doing what is necessary to make your dreams a reality.

The Fear of Failure

Fear of failure is one of the two major fears that you must work to overcome if you desire to accomplish anything of significance in your life. Carefully read the following symptoms of the fear of failure in order to determine how much of a hold it has over your decisions and actions.

Fear of failure has a hold on your life if you are:

- Indulging in the habit of perfectionism. You get lost in all the details in order to drag things on for as long as possible. As a result, you don't essentially get around to doing what is really important because you're afraid of failing.
- Feeling like losing control or essentially feeling powerless to take any sort of action that will move you a step closer to your desired outcomes.
- Trying to avoid failure at all costs and therefore spending time over-planning and essentially getting nowhere because your persistent and obsessive thoughts about failure are constantly getting in your way.
- Suffering from low self-esteem or low self-confidence. You simply don't believe in yourself or in your ability to become successful. As a result, you lack the willpower and discipline to do what is necessary to make your dreams a reality.
- In a state of uncontrollable worry and anxiety. You constantly worry about the unknown future. And because you don't know what could potentially happen, you fear that you might fail. And so you continue to worry about all the things that might go wrong. This paralyses you emotionally, and as a result, you make little progress.
- Unable to take risks or try new things. You may very well have big lofty goals, but if you are not

willing to step outside of your comfort zone, then this indicates that you are afraid of failing.

- Unable to commit wholeheartedly to the attainment of your goals and objectives. A lack of commitment indicates that there's some kind of fear holding you back from doing what is necessary to attain your desired outcomes. The most likely culprit is the fear of failure.

The Fear of Success

Fear of success is one of the two major fears that you must work to overcome if you desire to accomplish anything of significance in your life. Carefully read the following symptoms of the fear of success in order to determine how much of a hold it has over your decisions and actions.

Fear of success has a hold on your life if you are:

- Feeling as though you are not worthy or deserving of attaining your desired outcomes. This is mainly due to a set of irrational beliefs that are influencing your choices and decisions.
- Feeling guilty about achieving success or happiness. This again stems back to the fact that you don't feel you deserve to be successful or happy.
- Persistently indulging in destructive behaviour that is continuously sabotaging your progress. In such instances, you might very well make some huge strides along your journey, and then

suddenly you will do something really stupid that will prevent you from attaining your desired outcome. This is a clear indication of the fear of success manifesting in your life.

- Unable to make effective decisions. This stems back to the previous point about your self-sabotage patterns. During a pivotal moment along your journey, you will unconsciously sabotage yourself by making a silly decision that will take you off track.
- Not making enough effort on a daily basis to attain your desired outcomes. This might manifest as a lack of motivation, a lack of productivity or simply within your inability to organise yourself effectively.
- Indulging in the habit of procrastination. Even though you want to be successful, you procrastinate because unconsciously you are feeling comfortable with your life as it is at this very moment. You will, therefore, keep procrastinating in order to avoid doing what is necessary to achieve your end goal.

Imagining the negative consequences of success. Yes, of course, you want to achieve success, but the future isn't all rosy. There are consequences that you may not want, and this causes you to hesitate and doubt whether or not you really want to achieve your goal.

10 Insights to Help You Better Understand Your Fears

In order to win while playing a board game, or any game for that matter, it's important to first understand the rules. Once you understand the rules, you will be better able to make decisions throughout the game that will help you to improve your chances of winning. The same is true when it comes to your fears. You must learn to understand your fears before you can successfully overcome them.

Here are some critical things you need to understand about fear:

1. ***Fears Are Rooted in Childhood Experience***

Most of the fears you have today are actually rooted in childhood experience.

Back when you were a child things happened to you or to other people that brought about these fears. Maybe you were watching one of your parents experience a specific kind of fear, which you adopted as your own. Or maybe something significant occurred that left you feeling afraid and uncertain. No matter what it was, it left a lasting and significant impression on your brain and nervous system.

All this, of course, doesn't mean that this fear makes any rational sense at all. It might all just be in your imagination and may not even pose any physical danger or threat. However, at the time you accepted the fact that this experience was dangerous and painful and therefore it needed to be feared, and as a result, this created an irrational belief that you still hold onto till this day.

2. *Understanding the Impact of Your Fears*

Fear Results From a Lack of Something

The fears you experience in your life are there because you are lacking something in one or more of the following seven key areas:

First of all you simply don't know what to do or how to do things. In such instances ask yourself:

What don't I know?

What must I learn?

How will this help me?

You experience fear because you simply don't understand something. In such instances ask yourself:

What don't I understand?

Who could help me understand?

You experience fear because you lack proper perspective. In such instances ask yourself:

How do others see this?

How else could I perceive this situation?

How could this be of value?

You experience fear because you lack familiarity. In such instances ask yourself:

What am I unfamiliar with?

How can I become more familiar with this?

Who could potentially help me?

You experience fear because you lack the necessary experience when dealing with this particular situation. In such instances ask yourself:

What experience must I gain?

How will I gain this experience?

When will I gain this experience?

Who has this experience already and could potentially help me?

You experience fear because you lack the necessary resources to take action. In such instances ask yourself:

What resources do I need to get through this successfully?

Where will I find the necessary resources?

How will I acquire them?

Finally, you experience fear because you don't believe in your ability to take the necessary actions to attain your desired outcome. In such instances ask yourself:

What must I believe to do this successfully?

What must I believe to overcome this fear successfully?

You can use this list as somewhat of a checklist that can help you to progressively begin feeling more comfortable with your decisions and actions. In fact, by keeping these questions at the forefront of your mind throughout the day, will help you to think more rationally and thoughtfully about your fears. Who knows? This list could be all you need to begin creating positive momentum towards the attainment of your goals and objectives.

3. Fear Doesn't Like Change or Uncertainty

You are experiencing fear because there is some unknown element that is waiting for you around the corner. You don't know what is hiding there or what could potentially happen. This uncertainty stimulates your imagination and leads to uncontrollable irrational thoughts and beliefs that immediately lay down worst-case scenarios. This consequently creates even more uncertainty, and as a result, you become emotionally paralyzed — unable to take the necessary actions to get yourself out of this emotional mess.

The same is true when it comes to any kind of unexpected change. Life can change suddenly and rapidly. These changes can bring about uncertainty, and as a result, fear begins to creep into your life.

4. *Fears Are Part of the Human Experience*

Because life can often be uncertain and unpredictable, it's easy to see the value of fear. It's there as a protective mechanism that keeps us safe and helps us avoid potential pain.

This fear response has been ingrained in our psyche going back to our earliest ancestors who used fear as a survival mechanism that kept them alert and ready to fight or run at a moment's notice.

These days, while living in the big cities, we don't often confront animals who want to eat us for supper. However, even though this is true, fear does still have a place in life today — even in the big cities. But what's of primary importance today is that you don't get caught up in irrational fear where you lose all control and sense of reality. Instead, you must see fear for what it is: a protective mechanism — sometimes of an illusory nature — that you must understand and utilise to your advantage.

5. *Fear is Only Temporary if Challenged*

Have a think about all the fears you have experienced over a lifetime. I think it would be safe to say that you have overcome some of these fears successfully, while other fears have probably tended to hang around like a bad smell. The fact is, that the fears you overcame successfully were the fears that you challenged head-on. However, the fears that tend to persist in your life right now have probably never really been challenged — or at least you never really followed through completely with your actions.

Each of the fears you have in your life right now are only temporary if they are challenged. However, if they remain unchallenged, then they will continue to influence your choices and decisions until the moment you decide that things must change.

6, Fears Are a Warning Mechanism

Fear is nothing more than a warning mechanism of potential drawbacks, risks and negative consequences that might be waiting for you around the corner. These are of course all valid reasons to be wary and cautious, but not afraid. Being wary and cautious means that you think things through rationally and lay down an effective plan of action that will help you to minimise the risks and maximise the potential gains.

If on the other hand, you are making these decisions from a position of fear, then you will likely make irrational choices — most of which will be filled with excuses of why you shouldn't go through with your actions. Therefore it's absolutely critical that from this day onward, you are always wary and cautious, but never get caught up in fear.

7. How to Better Understand Your Fears

Fear Indicates You're About to Learn Something
Fear often presents you with a perfect opportunity for growth. When it crops up in your life, it's a clear indication that you better get ready because you're about to learn something new and different that could potentially change your life for the better. Therefore instead of resisting fear, embrace it and see it as an opportunity that can help you to grow exponentially as a person.

8. Fear Often Never Materialises

How many times has your fear actually materialised in the way that you imagined? Probably not very often. Maybe even, never! The reality is, that you will often imagine the consequences of your actions as being far worse than what is likely to happen. This creates increased levels of doubt and uncertainty, and as a result, you get caught up in your fears, and nothing positive happens.

Instead of fearing what could potentially happen, it's better to just expect that your fears will probably never even materialise, and if they do, they will never be as bad as you imagined. Hopefully, this can give you the confidence to begin moving beyond the fears that stand between you and the attainment of your goals and objectives.

9. You Can't Control Everything

Not only are you unable to control everything, you also will never know everything, and you will often never have all the information required that you need to eliminate the uncertainty you feel moving forward. And this is perfectly okay.

You don't need to know or control everything to venture into new territory. And you certainly don't need to wait for the perfect moment to take action, because there is never a perfect moment. But if there was a perfect moment, then that perfect moment would be right now. And stepping into the unknown is the perfect thing you can do because you will immediately begin to desensitise yourself from the experience the moment you decide to confront your fear head-on.

10. Fear is No Match for Bold Action

Whenever you take bold action towards your desired objectives consistently over time, you will progressively break down the walls of fear. This will help you to build courage and certainty. It will also lead to new perspectives, understandings, and knowledge as you continue to make progress along your journey – boosting your confidence along the way. Then eventually the discomfort you initially felt when you originally stepped into your fear will turn into comfort as you successfully expand your comfort zone.

Taking bold action and being willing to risk stepping into uncertainty is often the quickest and surest way to overcome all your fears.

CHAPTER 2

UNDERSTAND YOUR ANXIETIES

We frequently associate tension when we think of "anxiety."

Actually, anxiety is a response from our body to a threat to our safety. We wouldn't react in a dangerous situation without worry, and we probably wouldn't be here today either.

However, anxiety can encompass much more than just whether or whether we should flee a circumstance. Because of our innate will to survive, we tend to perceive more threats than there actually are, which might make us feel more apprehensive than is necessary.

The fact is that everybody has anxiety. Many people may find the anxiety to be intolerable. In the US, daily anxiety problems affect about 19% of adults.

A person is not weak if they experience anxiety or are diagnosed with an anxiety condition. They can overcome their anxieties and have happy, fulfilling lives with the correct support.

So What Exactly Is Anxiety?

Anxiety is our body's normal reaction to stress. When we're presented with potential danger, our bodies respond to that stress.

Fear is a similar emotional response. Fear is the body's response to a real or perceived imminent threat, and anxiety is our body—and mind—anticipating a future threat.

For example, if you're starting a new job, waiting for test results from a doctor, or driving in bad weather, you may feel anxious. This is a normal reaction to our emotions and happens to everyone. When anxiety stops being temporary fear or worry, it may be a sign that help is needed.

A person who has an anxiety disorder may always be anxious or easily become anxious about many things. Temporary fear or worry is normal, but if the feelings associated with anxiety disorders linger, they can continue to get worse over time.

Through understanding the condition and seeking the right treatment, anxiety can be managed.

Understanding the Many Anxiety Disorders—And Their Symptoms

While the phrase "I'm anxious" is spoken often, the type of anxiety that someone is experiencing can be hard to pinpoint. Many types of anxiety can impact everyday activities, like work, school, and relationships.

The following is not an exhaustive list of every disorder and symptom. If you feel that you or a loved one is experiencing any of the following, please reach out to your care providers to ensure that the right steps are being taken to support your mental health.

Generalised Anxiety Disorder

Generalised anxiety disorder **(GAD)** is extremely common, experienced by nearly one in eight people in the U.S.

GAD is known for a feeling of constant anxiety and worry about daily activities or events. This anxiety happens more days than not and occurs for at least six months.

Someone with GAD may feel as if they have no control over their worry or find themselves being overly concerned about money, health, family, work, or other daily occurrences. Sometimes, the thought of how to get through the day is enough to cause anxiety.

Many folks who have generalised anxiety disorder recognize that they are in a cycle of worry or that their anxiety is worse than the situation calls for. The challenge with GAD, though, is that the person doesn't know how to stop the cycle of worry or feels that it's out of their control.

Many people who are diagnosed with GAD also have co-occurring conditions, including depression, substance use, post-traumatic stress disorder (PTSD), and obsessive compulsive disorder (OCD).

Generalised anxiety disorder has both physical and mental symptoms, with most people experiencing some but not all symptoms. If you or someone you know is experiencing these symptoms, please reach out to your primary care provider or someone on your care team.

Physical symptoms include but are not limited to:

- Restlessness, feeling keyed up, or feeling on edge
- Feeling easily fatigued
- Muscle tension, aches, or soreness
- Sweating
- Accelerated heart rate, shortness of breath, or dizziness
- Stomach issues, including nausea and diarrhoea
- Trembling, twitching, feeling shaky
- Sleep disturbances, including difficulty falling or staying asleep or not feeling well-rested

Mental symptoms include but are not limited to:

- Excessive anxiety or worry about various events or activities, occurring more days than not, for at least six months
- Difficulty controlling the worry
- A sense of impending danger, panic, or doom

- Irritability
- Difficulty concentrating, or mind going blank
- Difficulty remembering things

- panic, or doom
- Irritability
- Difficulty concentrating, or mind going blank
- Difficulty remembering things

Panic Disorder
Panic disorder is a rush of anxiety that comes out of the blue that makes people feel like they're going crazy, having a heart attack, or going to die. Though it typically develops in folks between 18 and 35, it can occur at any time. Women are nearly twice as likely to develop panic disorder as men.

Unlike anxiety, which often has clear triggers, panic typically is sudden, uncontrollable fear or anxiety. This can often cause impulsive behaviour.

The fear response is one of the largest differentiators between panic disorder and other anxiety disorders. In panic disorder, the person is fearful of the fear they're feeling.

A person with panic disorder may feel terror even if there is no real danger. Many individuals with panic disorder have explained that their panic feels like they are losing control.

Panic happens quickly and unexpectedly and typically only lasts a few minutes. Anxiety tends to appear gradually and can last for extended periods.

Panic attacks can happen to anyone at any time. But people with panic disorder have recurring attacks, and they can't be explained by other mental health conditions.

Individuals with panic disorder will often change their behaviour related to attacks to try and avoid another attack from happening. They'll often be concerned or worried about additional panic attacks as well as the consequences—like feeling they are losing control or having a heart attack.

This constant concern and attempts at avoiding future attacks can majorly impact areas of the person's life. It can lead to the development of additional mental health issues, like agoraphobia, which is a fear of being in certain places or situations, such as being in a crowd.

Some physical symptoms of panic disorder include:

- Rapid heartbeat or a pounding heart
- Sweating
- Trembling or shaking
- Chest pain
- Shortness of breath
- Dizziness, unsteadiness, or lightheadedness
- Stomach distress

Some of the mental symptoms of panic include:

- Feeling detached from oneself or reality
- Fear of losing control
- Fear of dying
- Feelings of impending doom

Social Anxiety Disorder

People with social anxiety disorder experience a dread of being evaluated or ashamed in public settings. Frequently, they will put up with extreme feelings of fear or worry while dealing with a social scenario. If the social phobia persists for at least six months, this might be regarded as an anxiety disorder.

Social anxiety disorder is thought to affect 7% of Americans, with older groups having a lower prevalence of the condition.

Adolescent girls and women are diagnosed with it slightly more frequently. The majority of persons begin to exhibit symptoms between the ages of eight and fifteen.

The worry that one will receive a poor judgement from others is one of the defining characteristics of social anxiety. Frequently, the person fears being perceived as nervous, feeble, unintelligent, dull, unlikable, or possessing some other unfavourable quality.

With this disease, being perceived poorly in social circumstances virtually always results in worry or anxiety that is frequently disproportionate to the actual risk. Many people who struggle with social anxiety may repeatedly try to avoid being in social situations.

Some of the symptoms of a social anxiety disorder include:

- Fear or anxiety about one or more social situations where the person is exposed to possible scrutiny by others
- Shyness or being withdrawn in social situations
- Blushing
- Sweating
- Being closed off in conversation or revealing very little about oneself
- Trembling or shaking
- Overly rigid body posture
- Poor eye contact
- Softly speaking
- Stumbling over one's words
- Staring

In children, additional physical symptoms include:

- Crying
- Tantrums
- Freezing in place
- Clinging to a parent or guardian
- Shrinking back
- Refusal to speak in social situations

Separation Anxiety
Some anxiety about separating from loved ones is normal. Separation anxiety disorder is excess concern, dread, or worry about actual or anticipated separation from someone a person is emotionally attached to. Separation anxiety is a common anxiety disorder in kids but is also present in adults.

Attachment figures for children are usually adults, such as parents. In adults, this could be any loved one, from a romantic partner to a child, or even a pet. Typically, the individual is afraid that something bad will happen to the person they care about while they're not present.

Separation anxiety disorder can have a huge impact on all areas of life. In adults, it can lead to social isolation, inability to work, or relationship troubles.

Phobias
Phobias are fears of objects or situations which can be disruptive to a person's life. Some more common phobias are:

- *Hemophobia (fear of blood*)
- *Trypanophobia (fear of needles or medical procedures involving injections/hypodermic needles)*
- *Agoraphobia (fear of places or situations that might cause panic/feeling trapped, helpless, or embarrassed)*

Fear associated with phobias is usually present for six months or longer. Depending on the type of phobia, they can be disruptive to daily life activities, such as going to work, travelling, and socialising.

Obsessive Compulsive Disorder

Obsessive compulsive disorder (OCD), frequently regarded as an anxiety disorder, is a condition in which a person has intrusive and unwanted thoughts. Feelings of apprehension, uncertainty, and occasionally panic follow these thoughts.

This illness is much more than sporadic obsessional thoughts or behaviours. The person may battle obsessions or compulsions on a daily basis if they have OCD.

OCD patients experience a cycle of obsessions and compulsions that affect their thought processes and actions.

These cycles can have an effect on many parts of their personal, academic, social, and professional lives if the disease is left untreated.

Between the ages of 8 and 12, as well as in late adolescence or early adulthood, OCD typically initially manifests. OCD affects an estimated two to three million individuals in the United States and affects people of all sexes, races, nationalities, and socioeconomic backgrounds equally.

The mere presence of an obsession or compulsion does not indicate OCD in a person.

In general, OCD sufferers:

- Spend at least one hour each day addressing compulsions or obsessions.
- experience compulsions and obsessions that interfere with daily living and/or relationships.
- Cannot control their thoughts or behaviours, even when they negatively affect daily life, and only feel relief from anxiety while engaging in a compulsion that doesn't provide them pleasure

Most people occasionally have invasive, unwelcome ideas. However, in OCD, these ideas result in a severe reaction that interferes with daily functioning and activities.

What Motivates Fear?

Nearly one-third of Americans will develop an anxiety disorder at some point in their lives. The illnesses can manifest at any time, even though they are frequently diagnosed in the early adolescent years.

Anxiety has a biological foundation. Neurotransmitters are brain molecules that convey instructions about how we should feel. People may be more prone to feeling anxious if they are not communicating the proper information at the appropriate time.

Research has revealed that an increased chance of getting an anxiety disorder might result from both genetic and environmental variables. There are a variety of risks for acquiring anxiety disorders, such as but not limited to:

- exposure to traumatic experiences in adolescence or adulthood

Anxiety or other mental diseases run in the family
Childhood episodes of shyness that are unpredictable
The signs of anxiousness might sometimes get worse due to certain health issues. Anxiety symptoms can be induced or made more severe by a heart arrhythmia, coffee consumption, or drug adverse effects.

CHAPTER 3

Understanding Worry

How Is Worry Defined?

Any bad emotions, pictures, ideas, or concerns that are triggered by current issues or problems in the future, whether they be genuine or imagined.

How does this compare to what you meant by that?

Of course, the following wide definition covers a lot of ground! This may be worrying about a forthcoming operation, your finances, or the future of your children. You'll probably discover that it fits this description of worry if you quickly consider something that is worrying you right now.

Determine Your Concerns

Ask yourself if this worry is a thought, feeling, image, or something else; if it is negative in character; and whether it is real or imagined as you continue to visualise it. In truth, it's far more difficult to accomplish than it initially appears.

It's not always easy to determine if something is actually likely to occur or not. Imagine, for instance, that one day you discover a brand-new, incredibly odd-looking mole on your back that, in your opinion, appears to be quite harmful. You start to worry since so many members of your extended family have skin cancer and wonder if you might be next.

Sometimes worries are focused in the future and are concerns about what might possibly occur. However, not all of the things we worry about are equally likely to occur. And even when there is a good possibility that something will occur, thinking about it frequently has no effect on altering the outcome.

How Likely Is It?

Look at the following worrying thoughts, and decide whether the fear is real or imaginary. In other words, how likely the fear is to come true.

- You get a rare form of cancer from eating some expired food in your fridge and will die within a month.
- The person who is late and hasn't texted you back has been in a horrible car accident.
- You won't have enough money saved up for retirement.
- People are talking behind your back.
- Your spouse is cheating or will eventually.

If you hesitated with some of these, it's understandable. Naturally, it is more difficult to decide if something is real or imaginary, when you are already worrying about it.

Do You Have Any Control?

However, refraining from asking how likely something is to occur is a smart place to start when trying to moderate and manage your fear. After all, all of the aforementioned scenarios are theoretically and hypothetically possible. Ask how much power you actually have over the circumstance instead. We'll examine methods for doing this in greater detail in part three of this course, but for now, consider the above ideas again and see if your responses to the question "How much influence do I have over whether or not this happens?" have changed.

How does this affect the way you perceive the ideas presented above?

How Much Worry Is Too Much Worry?

Check out this Ten(10) outcomes of worry

1. Feeling so worried about your finances that you buy a money management book.
2. Worrying so much that you throw up before an important speech you're supposed to give.

3. Falling asleep at 3 am in the morning because you were worrying about all the things that could go wrong the following day.
4. Declining to go home with a blind date because you have a bad feeling about them.
5. Staying at work an extra hour because you're worried about a difficult project you're working on.
6. Staying at work an extra 2 hours for a week because you're worried about a difficult project you're working on.
7. Turning in the project late because you're worrying about it made you procrastinate.
8. Taking over-the-counter pain medication every day to deal with the stress and worries of raising a young family.
9. Going to the doctor because of a persistent health condition you're worried about.
10. Calling the police to report suspicious activity happening in your neighbourhood.

Adaptive and Maladaptive Worry

Not all worries are bad, neither is worrying the same for everyone. It's crucial to define worry for yourself personally in order to take control of your life and comprehend how it impacts you.

Different Views on the Same Situation

Going back to our skin cancer example, you might start to worry a lot, schedule a doctor's appointment, and worry for days as you read frightful things online to make yourself more and more concerned. Alternately, you may schedule the appointment and promptly forget about it. Most likely nothing will happen.

Stress is a result of an interaction between an organism and its environment rather than just an external input. The ability of an organism to respond to a stimulus successfully determines whether or not it is considered stressful. So rather than saying "this unusual mole is frightening," it would be more realistic to state "I find this weird mole worrying."

Worry Has Several Faces

In order to handle worry, people are frequently advised to decompress, unwind, perhaps listen to some whale music, and practice meditation. You probably know someone who would sooner pass away than do any of this and who would actually find the entire experience to be quite distressing. We rarely mean "concern" in the sense of just one thing because each of us has unique personal resources, coping mechanisms, and ways of understanding the world.

Is Your Personal Worry Too Much?

So, answering the question (how much worry is too much worry?) becomes a little easier. A good yardstick to use is this: is worry interfering with your ability to grow, connect with others, satisfy work and family obligations and generally do what you need to do in your life? If so, then this can be considered "too much" worry, or maladaptive worry. If, on the other hand, your worry is making you feel motivated, inspired and ready to act, then it's more likely adaptive worry – no matter what that worry happens to be.

Applied to the Real World

In the real world, this means that there is allowance for our individual differences. A massive deadline in 12 hours could make a thriving Wall Street trader roll up his sleeves and accept the challenge, whereas the same might make a sleep-deprived new mother want to pull out her hair.

Sources of Stress

Even when you know you are feeling worried, it may often be challenging to recognize the exact sources of stress that are affecting you. Considering some specific details of your life, and the extent to which they cause you to worry, will help you understand yourself and your personal needs.

Not Right or Wrong - Just Personal

Of course, there's no right or wrong way to do this, because it is a way to start becoming aware of your own mental resources and your own personal resilience when it comes to stress and worry.

- Speaking in front of a crowd
- Travelling somewhere you've never been before
- Having a tight budget, or being in debt

- Thinking about tasks you still have to do
- Being rushed
- Feeling guilty that you have or haven't done what was expected
- Feeling unsure about how a situation will turn out
- Worries that you're being judged
- Thinking about tasks you haven't done yet
- Thoughts about random events like accidents or illnesses happening to you
- Thoughts about global warming, pollution or endangered animals
- Feelings about a family member's safety
- Doing new things
- Regretting things that have already been done
- Worries about your health or the health of someone you love
- Worrying that something bad will happen
- Worries about whether you'll be good enough for a role you've been given
- Stress about exam and school performance
- Stressing about things being clean and orderly
- Feeling unprepared for a task
- Vague worries that you aren't living the life you should be
- Feelings that romantic partners don't return your affections
- Worries about being so much more worried than everyone else.
- Worries about nothing in particular!

If you have them, add some worries of your own as well.

If you have someone nearby who's willing, ask them to go through the same list and compare – are there any surprising patterns?

Specific or General?

Are you worried about one, two things or just life in general? If you've noticed anything noteworthy, put it down now in your journal. You might also like to note whether your worry seems to "float" and be about everything and nothing at all.

Ways of Thinking About Worry

Now that you have begun to understand worry, it is time to review what we have learned so far, as well as to talk about what is going to happen next. Most importantly, it is all about your personal experience of stress and worry.

What's Next?

In this section, we'll dig a little deeper and try to understand why people worry in the first place. Once we do this, we'll have a clearer understanding about how to gradually take control of our mental health and worry less.

Take It Personally

But, we have already seen that when it comes to worry, no two people are built the same. Since we all face life's challenges with a unique set of skills and weaknesses, we're all likely to explain and understand our own stressful thoughts a little differently. Take a moment now to try to answer the question: "Why do I worry so much?"

Consider the Possibilities

Give yourself a few minutes to quickly jot down whatever comes to mind, then look at the explanations in the next few chapters, that some theorists have suggested, to explain why people worry. Do any of them resonate with you?

Eustress and Distress

You might be shocked to learn that not all tension is unhealthy for you as the word "stress" is frequently associated with negative connotations. While some forms of stress can make you feel nervous and unmotivated, others may inspire you to make improvements in your life.

What Conditions Cause Stress?

Importantly, this is a property in how a person evaluates and responds to a situation rather than a trait of the stimuli itself. Therefore, regardless of how uncomfortable the stimuli appears to others, a situation might be categorised as stressful or disturbing if a person lacks the psychological capacity to deal with it.

Eustress, or constructive stress

Eustress is any difficult stimuli that stresses the person but also makes them feel energised, driven, or forced to react or do some sort of self-help activity.

What Effects Can Stress Have on Your Life?

Eustress can therefore be compared to the stress of healthy rivalry or competitiveness, to the controllable anxiety of an upcoming exam (which prompts the person to prepare harder), or to a "wake up call" that prompts someone to leave a harmful situation or make significant adjustments to their way of life. In other words, eustress has a direct or indirect beneficial effect.

Unfavourable/Stress{distress}

Contrarily, distress occurs when stress, trauma, anxiety, and concern are unproductive and drive the person to shut down rather than motivate healthy activity. Stress that paralyses a person in dread, impairs their capacity for thought, prevents them from working well, hinders their ability to communicate with people or fulfil their daily tasks is not beneficial stress. Stress is directly or indirectly harmful and so problematic when it leads to less action.

What About You?

What do you think? Does this theory ring true when you think about your own worry?

Mindfulness

Worried minds are seldom able to focus on what is happening right now. Anxiety usually dissects either the past or the future and that gets in the way of happiness.

Mindfulness

To counter this, most schools of Buddhism today encourage mindful awareness, and the understanding that what goes on in the mind is not necessarily reality, and is not the self. Through meditative practices, practitioners can learn to detach from a busy, ego-filled mind and attain a sense of serenity.

Where Does Worry Occur?

When you think about it, worry always lives somewhere outside the present moment. Either we worry about what has already happened in the past, or we worry about what might still happen in the future. The result? We are never truly in the present moment.

The Solution

Try and cultivate a deeper appreciation for the moment, i.e. being more aware and alert to your surroundings, as well as learning to detach a little from busy and overactive thoughts. We'll look a little more closely at techniques to combat mindlessness in part three of this course.

What About You?

What do you think? Does this theory ring true when you think about your own worry?

Mental Resources

Worry and negative stress can also be the result of the relationship between what is happening to you, or the situation you are in, and the resources you feel you have, in order to deal with it.

How to Cope?

When our inner resources are greater than our environmental worries, then we can be said to cope. Coping is also a learned skill, and something we can develop. We use the skills and attitudes we need to survive and even thrive in adversity. The solution suggested by this theory is obvious: find a way to increase your personal resources.

Worry and the Feeling of Powerlessness

A variation on this theory is that worry can be an expression of powerlessness. When you are able to perceive something unpleasant but are prevented somehow from doing anything about it, you may experience worry. This explains the kind of worry mothers feel when their young children insist on climbing dangerous looking trees – they keenly feel that they ought to do something, but also that they are powerless and that kids will be kids and occasionally do reckless things.

What About You?

What do you think? Does this theory ring true when you think about your own worry?

An Evolutionary Perspective

Another theory to consider is that in many ways, worry is useful. This may sound ludicrous to you, but let's think about how humans have evolved over the centuries, and how the environment we live in has changed.

According to this perspective, stress and worry evolved in the human species because it was beneficial. Knowing how to respond to potentially dangerous threats in the environment was a good skill for our ancestors to have. Those early ancestors who were reckless daredevils would not have lived long enough to pass on their genes, and so in time the more cautious, worry-prone genes were preserved in future generations.

Worrying - Past and Present

The trouble is, the environment humans evolved in is very different from the one we inhabit now. In the past, a jolt of adrenaline and cortisol would be just the right thing to flee dangers like lethal animals and hazardous situations. Today, most of us have never and will never encounter a potential fall off a cliff or a sabre-toothed tiger.

Modern Worries
Modern man instead experiences more abstract worries like relationship troubles, credit card debt, toxic friends, unfulfilling work, existential fears and anxieties... the trouble is our bodies are still designed to respond in the same way as our ancient ancestors. When you feel your heart rate increase and your chest tighten in a stressful situation, you're experiencing a physical fight or flight response that saved many of your ancestor's lives. Most of us, though, wish we could control these automatic responses a little better.

What About You?

What do you think? Does this theory ring true when you think about your own worry?

A Holistic Perspective

Finally, worry may have a much simpler explanation. This theory posits that it may be the result of negative influences to the human organism. If that is the case, then you probably already know what the solution may be.

Our final theory is one that might be more familiar to you. This theory simply states that worry (and stress, anxiety etc.) all arise as a result of imbalance and general lack of wellbeing. For this way of thinking, the human being is a complex organism, the health of which relies on the health of several interlocking systems.Our final theory is one that might be more familiar to you. This theory simply states that worry (and stress, anxiety etc.) all arise as a result of imbalance and general lack of wellbeing. For this way of thinking, the human being is a complex organism, the health of which relies on the health of several interlocking systems.

When Does Worry Occur?

This means that worry is more likely when nutrition or sleep quality is poor, when there is a lack of social support, when work or relationships are unfulfilling, or when the person is forced to endure an unsupportive environment.

What's the Solution?

Here, worry can have emotional, physical, cultural, even spiritual components. When worry is understood this way, the solution appears to be to balance the entire person's sense of wellbeing across all areas.

What About You?

What do you think? Does this theory ring true when you think about your own worry?

What Worry Means to You

You now have a decent amount of knowledge about worrying. As important as that it is, it is always most decisive to understand what worry means to you personally and to set goals that will motivate you.

What Worries You?

Ask yourself the questions listed below, to get a clearer understanding of what worry means to you personally.

What is your personal definition of worry?

What worries you particularly?

What is the biggest worry of all?

How much do you worry – too much?

Go Back to the Theories

What causes your worry? You can refer to the theories mentioned in the previous chapters (the evolutionary theory, the mindfulness theory etc.) or you can use your own explanation.

Ready to Set Some Goals?

Hopefully you are, because now that you've got a slightly deeper understanding of how you think about your worry, let's start making some goals!

Taking Charge of Your Anxiety

You are off to a great start! Now that you have learned so much, it is time to get ready and take things into your own hands

CHAPTER 4

Stress Test – Part 1

How Are You Holding Up?

Let's take a quick look into your stress levels and make sure you are doing well emotionally.Stop. Take a deep breath. Relax your entire body and try to clear your mind for a moment. How are you feeling?

Do any of the words below describe you at the moment?

- Curious
- Bored
- Tired
- Angry
- Stressed
- Cynical
- Neutral
- Optimistic
- Calm
- Confident
- Fearful
- Embarrassed
- Irritated
- Sad
- Overwhelmed
- Nervous
- Excited

Are there any you'd like to add? Jot them down.

Stress Test – Part 2

How Are You Holding Up?

For some of us, the last time we were truly relaxed and unstressed was when we were children. Before work and family obligations, uncertainties about the future or worry about life in general began to eat away at our mental wellbeing, most of us were remarkably well adjusted.

How Are You?

When it comes to dealing with everyday worries, how are you holding up?

Below you'll find a quick quiz to take a reading of your current stress levels and coping mechanisms. Once you have an idea of your current situation, it'll be easier to apply some of the stress-management techniques that follow.

Try Taking the Quiz

Decide if your answer is either "yes" or "no" for each statement. It is crucial to be honest - after all, you are doing this for you, the results are private and will help you going forward.

- *I have a supportive group of friends and family I can turn to when things get difficult.*

- *I seldom get colds and flus.*
- *I generally feel calm, organised and in control of my life.*
- *I know when I'm feeling overwhelmed and have to take a step back to gather my thoughts before continuing with the day's activities.*
- *I sleep well and usually for around 7 or 8 hours a night, most nights.*
- *I generally complete the tasks I assign myself every day.*
- *I use my leisure time well and have hobbies I enjoy.*
- *I know when to say "no" to a task I know I can't realistically do.*
- *I have time for myself every day where I just sit, read, reflect or meditate.*
- *I have something to look forward to in my future.*
- *Other people's opinions are important to me, but in the end I make my own decisions and go my own way.*
- *I don't enjoy my work 100% of the time, but I am satisfied in general.*
- *I feel like I have effective ways of dealing with life's minor irritations.*
- *All considered, I don't have too many regrets about the past.*
- *I live a generally healthy lifestyle, eat well and exercise.*

Results

If You Answered "Yes" to All 15

Congratulations, you're keeping on top of the worries life throws your way and have stress management skills in place that keep you grounded and in control.

If You Answered "Yes" to 10 – 15

You probably have a good handle on daily stressors, but occasionally have a specific weak spot that causes worry and anxiety, for example work or relationships. The challenge for you will be to develop worry management skills in this particular area.

If You Answered "Yes" to 5 – 10

You could definitely benefit from taking stock of your current worry management techniques and finding ways to better support yourself. Whether you need to actively seek to reduce the sources of worry in your life, find better ways to cope with inevitable stress or both will depend on your unique life situation.

If You Answered "Yes" to 5 or Fewer

Worry has clearly gotten the better of you and is threatening to damage your quality of life and wellbeing. Stress at this level is typically not sustainable, and you may find that serious changes are in order.

What Were These Questions About?

In the quiz you've just completed, you might have noticed that some of the items were not about your external world alone and how stressful it may or may not be. Rather, the statements were concerned with how you interpreted the stressors in your life. Since anxiety and worry are a result of how changes in our environment are perceived, it makes sense to start there when trying to reduce the amount of stress and worry.

Now What?

Well, no matter what your current situation, there are always ways to improve on your general wellbeing, specifically the way you tackle the worries of everyday life. Read on for how you can start to develop techniques to enhance your own resilience against worry.

CHAPTER 5

Self-Inventory

Keeping a Worry Journal

As you move through the rest of this course, it will be incredibly useful to keep a record of your progress. Sometimes, it does feel as though you are standing still or even moving backwards – but a regularly updated journal can remind you just how far you've come and inspire you to keep going.

A worry journal allows you to see patterns that may have been hidden otherwise. When you understand your larger cycles and rhythms, you get to understand your mind in a much deeper, more nuanced way.
What to Write in Your Worry Journal?
It's up to you! But here are some ideas you might like to try:

Start every day with a brief write up of how you're feeling and how you plan to tackle the challenges of the day ahead.

Literally put all your worries down on paper. It's amazing how simply writing something down can subtly change your perspective on it.
For a few days, closely monitor your stress levels. Set an alarm on your phone and when it goes off, take a moment to rate your worry levels on a scale of 1 to 10. Over a few days, you'll start to notice interesting patterns emerging.
Keep a log of your daily, weekly and monthly goals. Writing down your intentions can further cement them in your mind.
When to Write
When it comes to journaling, it's best to be regular and consistent.

After a few weeks, go back to your first few entries – you'll be surprised at how much has changed!

Cultivating Resilience

Portrait of a Resilient Person

Being your unique self is always most important, but having a positive example to inspire change in your life can also be helpful. You too can be the image of a resilient, calm person!

Quick, close your eyes and think of someone you know and admire for their ability to never worry too much or become overwhelmed with fear. If you can't think of someone real, a fictional or movie character is OK, too, or you could imagine a person composed of elements from separate people you know.

Important Qualities

Now, ask yourself what qualities this person possesses. Do they:

- Have a ridiculous sense of humour
- Never seem to rush
- Seem to have deep inner calm about life in general
- Have some spiritual or religious conviction that seems to strengthen them
- Participate in calming hobbies like meditation or long walks
- Know how to have fun
- Know how to laugh at themselves
- Know how to put up with uncertainty without being stressed by the unknown
- Step away from unnecessarily stressful situations
- Have a support network to help them through difficulty

What else can you add to that list?

How Does That Relate to You?

In your journal, pick just one or two of these characteristics and make a small goal for yourself to nurture that characteristic in your own personality. If you admire someone's ability to always be able to laugh at themselves instead of worrying about failure, for example, set yourself a goal to achieve that.

How to Do It?
If you have chosen, as a goal, to learn to laugh at yourself, deliberately do something a little scary or outside your comfort zone, find the funny aspects of the situation and laugh at yourself, whatever the outcome.

If you admire someone's commitment to their meditation practice, vow to meditate for twenty minutes today, and actually do it.

Developing Your Own Strategy

As you've probably noticed, the focus on this course has been you, and how you can develop skills and techniques to combat your own particular brand of worry. Now it is time to focus on your specific goals and strategies.

What Now?
In the chapters that follow, you will find some hands-on tools and techniques that you can use. You don't have to use all of them, but experimenting is always encouraged.

How Should You Start?
A recommended strategy is to make an entry in your worry journal every day to keep track of your progress, the exercises you've done, what worked and what didn't. It's also a good place to keep your goals and track your

improvements. Beyond that, how you use your worry journal is up to you!

What to Add to Your Journal

Collect and paste pictures from magazines, write down persistent thoughts, poetry, articles you find interesting, sketches, anything really. As you move through the following exercises, jot down things that stand out to you and any goals or questions they inspire.

Take Charge!

By taking charge of your own process and your own healing, you get to add your own personal touch to your worry management strategy.

CHAPTER 6

Technique 1 : Mindfulness

Mindfulness and Meditation

The first technique we'll consider to help boost our personal resilience and help combat stress is mindful awareness. It has been used for thousands of years by different cultures, and so it is worth looking into, as something that may be helpful to you as well.

Mindfulness has long been in the repertoire of healers and therapists, who understand the importance of the mind/body connection. There is a wealth of information available for the casual student of mindfulness, and several different schools of thought in Eastern philosophical traditions that emphasise different aspects of this practice.

Mindfulness vs. Worry

For the purposes of everyday stress and worry, it's largely sufficient to approach mindfulness as a method that promotes tranquillity, awareness and a sense of calm detachment from the chaos of the mind.

What Is Mindfulness About?

Common to all traditions is the root understanding that the mind is not the self, and that thoughts about reality are not to be confused with the actual reality. This fundamental principle opens a space in which stressful, overwhelming or irrational thoughts can be seen for what they are, and let go. As you can imagine, this framework is highly compatible with other psychological treatment modalities, such as cognitive behavioural therapy.

How to Apply Mindfulness?

To foster a more resilient sense of awareness, people are encouraged to meditate or engage in other exercises that deliberately ask the person to become aware of the present moment and all the contents of their mind. This is often the first step to being able to moderate and control thoughts.

Let's Imagine It!

A common analogy is to imagine that the mind is clear and unchanging like a blue sky, and thoughts are merely clouds and weather passing through – in other words, they will both pass. The principle of non-attachment asks practitioners to stop identifying with temporary thoughts as this only causes suffering. Instead, a sense of peace is achieved and some distance gained, even when thoughts become difficult and unpleasant.

Mindfulness Can Help You Focus

Mindfulness exercises can also bring the wandering mind back to the present moment, which works well because a stressed and anxious mind often lives in either the past or the future. Simple breathing meditations keep focus and awareness of the breath, the sensations of the body in the present moment as it unfolds, and the fleeting thoughts that enter into and leave the mind.

Why Should You Try It?

Ultimately, the goal is to create the ability to access a calm, alert and aware state of mind throughout life. Anecdotal reports suggest that anxiety responds well to mindfulness practice, and research has backed up some of these claims. Those who meditate have been shown to have less stress and report a greater sense of balance and wellness.

You Can Practice Right Now!

Notice the weight of your limbs and how it feels for your body to touch the chair.

Listen to the sounds around you and notice what thoughts you have about them.

Try not to judge any of those thoughts, just let them come and then go again.

Become aware of any aches, pains, tension or strange pulls in your body. You can choose to relax these if you like.

Notice thoughts that come up and watch them as though somebody else was having them. Notice how easy it is to get carried away with and distracted by some thoughts. Let them go anyway.

Come back to your breath. Notice the rhythm. Simply be aware.

Success Will Follow

You may only be able to tolerate a few moments of this, and that's OK. You don't need to sit on a cushion and chant, and you certainly don't need to berate yourself if you find you're incredibly distracted or even bored. The important thing is that you keep trying! Your sense of alert awareness will grow with time.

CHAPTER 7

Technique 2: Visualisation 1

Visualisation is much more potent than you might have ever thought. Your imagination can have profound, very real effects on your physical and mental wellbeing.

Imagine It Like It's Real

Take a moment to imagine a nice, juicy lemon in real life, right now. Picture how it smells as you bring it closer to your face, how it's cool, waxy peel feels on your fingertips, its bright, fresh yellow colour and the way the light catches each of its tiny cells.

Include All Your Senses

Now, imagine you're bringing it closer to you and into your mouth, onto your tongue, and immediately tasting the sharp – almost electric! – feel the citric acid hitting your taste buds. Take a moment to really imagine your face curling up from the sour taste.

Physical Reactions to Imagined Incentive

Now, if you've really imagined this in depth, you may notice something – you actually begin to salivate. It's as if your body really did encounter a real lemon. Your taste buds, responding to the contents of your mind, prepared themselves for a lemon that wasn't really there. Your body, in other words, doesn't know the difference between the real and imagined lemon.

Why Is This Important for Worrying?

Your imagination forms the bridge between the unreal and the real, and an imaginary vision of a lemon can have real, tangible results in your body. When you stress, you take an unreal image and turn it into the real release of cortisol and adrenaline (stress hormones) in your body. This translates to real muscle aches, real injuries, real loss of sleep, real headaches and eventually, real illness.

This is why positive and relaxing visualisation can be so powerful – by imagining peaceful states of mind, we literally bring them into being.

Technique 2: Visualisation 2

As you now know, visualisation can have powerful effects on your mind and body, which is why it is also an excellent tool to use when you want to achieve something specific, such as leading a calmer life.

Include Your Full Imagination

In the same way that you visualised all the details about the lemon, visualise the details of that scene.Close your eyes and imagine that you are immersed in it. Consult each of your senses.

Focus on the Details

Below are some questions to help you create a more detailed, realistic scene, in your imagination.

- What can you smell in this place?
- What do you see? Look carefully around at every tiny detail
- What sensations can you feel on your skin? How hot or cold are you? What do your feet feel as they stand on the ground?
- What can you hear?
- What can you taste?
- How do you feel in this place? Imagine your facial expression. What thoughts are you having? Imagine colours, images and symbols that match this emotion
- What are you doing? Imagine how it feels to move your body in this place; take a moment to absorb every detail

How to Use it?

You can take this visualisation anywhere you like. You could spend 5 minutes each day recreating your tranquil world, and return back to it at stressful moments throughout the day.

Go Further

You could also extend the meditation slightly and imagine a glowing, healing ball of light that fills your body. Try imagining your stress as particles that evaporate off of you and float into the air, or picture a friend and guide in your special place who you tell your troubles to. It's your visualisation. What you do really depends on you.

What's the Point?
The main thing is that you use the power of your mind to bring about healing and relaxing changes in your body. Keep breathing. Take note of any tension and pain in your body and let it go.

This is an excellent practice to develop for just before bedtime and will guarantee restful dreams.

Technique 3: DIY CBT

A very popular psychological framework to understand and tackle anxiety is CBT, or the Cognitive Behavioural Therapy approach. A licensed professional can help tackle your worries using this framework, but you can use some of the fundamental principles yourself, right now, on your own.

To begin, open a computer file where you could write, or if you prefer - take a piece of paper and a pencil/pen. Ready?
Let's Go!
List 5 or 6 of your main worries in life at the moment. They can be anything from money worries to stress about a breakup, conflict with colleagues at work, or anxiety about a health problem.

Connect Your Worries to Your Thoughts

Take a moment to list 5 or 6 thoughts to correspond with each problem. What thoughts typically come up for you when you worry about this problem? Spend some time on this. The thing we're looking for is that thought that instantly makes your body tense up and merely thinking of it makes you feel bad.

How to Write Your Thoughts Down

Now, put these thoughts down. You could write, "I'm not making enough money and I'm going to end up destitute" or "She was my last chance for happiness, I'll never find love again" or "My colleagues all think I'm an idiot."

What About Your Behaviour?

Chances are, these thoughts are going to be very negative and uncomfortable – but that's OK. You've looked at the "cognitive" part of the equation, what about the "behavioural" part? Well, take some time to think of the way you behave as a result of these thoughts you've put down. Do you stay at home and sulk? Stop taking risks? Procrastinate?

As you can probably see, the cost of having these thoughts is often quite high. If you wish to change the resulting behaviour, you'll need to get to the root and change the thoughts that make the behaviour possible.

What Can You Do?

With that in mind, your next goal is to try to moderate these statements so that they are more in line with reality. In other words, you're going to argue with yourself on these assumptions. Look for absolute statements ("always" and "never") which are just not realistically possible, and look for overly negative sentiments or thoughts where you've made assumptions that may not be true.

Question Your Thoughts

Below are some helpful questions you can use to examine your negative thoughts.

- Is your statement really true?
- Is it true all the time?
- Hasn't there been a time when it wasn't true?
- Is the statement true but only partially?
- Have you exaggerated?
- What positive information are you ignoring in this statement?

Change It Up!

You might change the statement "I'll never find love again" to a more realistic one: "It's possible that I will never find love again, but more likely that I will, provided I put myself out there and am open to it."

What's the Worst that Can Happen?

Even if your statement is awful and happens to be true, carry it to its fullest conclusion. Let's say it really is true that you'll never find love again, worst case scenario.

Is it really so bad?
Is your life over, or can you derive lots of meaning and fulfilment from happy friendships, challenging work and a million other things? Even if you never had another relationship, is it really the end of the world anyway?

What to Do From Now On
The next time you catch yourself having a negative or unrealistic thought, deliberately remind yourself to replace it with a more realistic, less stressful one that is more likely to lead to productive actions. You don't have to lie to yourself or be overly optimistic, but often the thoughts that stress us are already distorted and an exercise like this merely corrects that.

Technique 4: Stoicism

A Stoic Trick for a Tranquil Mind
On our quest to be more resilient, we now move onto the Stoics. The ancient Stoics had a life philosophy that may seem alien to our modern sentiments, but nevertheless holds some interesting perspectives on how to deal with stress today.

Let's take a quick look at a way to approach life's problems, as the Stoics thought people should. You may even see the commonalities between this ancient approach and modern CBT methods, one of which you've already encountered.

How to Begin

Take a moment to think of a life problem, a worry or a thing that gives you anxiety at the moment. Now, according to the Stoics, life problems like these fall into only one of three categories, and the category it falls into determines how you can deal with it. Keeping your problem in mind, consider categories.

Category One

Things that you have full control over – these include your response to a situation, what you do or say and your thoughts about an event.

Example: whether you tell a colleague that you won't lie to management about their behaviour is a choice entirely up to you and 100% within your control.

Category Two

Things you have only partial control over – these include grey areas and situations that you can sway or influence, but not completely.

For example, you could make amends and apologise to a friend you've insulted, but whether they forgive you or not is not in your control – it's in theirs.

Category Three

Things you have no control over – these include things like the weather; if you'll have a car accident or not; the country you happened to be born in, etc.

For example, whether you are born male or female is 100% out of your control.

Your Problems

Now, go back to the list of problems you initially created, and think about which category each of them falls under. For each problem choose only one category.

Category One Problems

Super! You have complete control over your problem. So, turn whatever stress you have on the issue into the best possible action, given your circumstances. Here, worry and anxiety can be used as essential motivation to act wisely. Think carefully about your goals and options, weigh them up, and act. Here, worry is entirely unnecessary. Merely act concurrently and adjust.

Category Two Problems

Great! Your problem is partly under your control. Your challenge now is deciding what aspects you can influence and what aspects you can't. In our example, your stress and anxiety are best channelled into apologising and making sure you don't offend your friend in that way again. But what about those aspects you don't have control over? Well, then those aspects belong to category three.

Category Three Problems

Congratulations! There's not a thing you can do about your problem. This may seem glib, but when you think about it, it is incredibly freeing, as well. If a problem cannot be controlled by you, it doesn't matter what you do, it will continue to be whatever it is. In this case, you might as well let it go and free yourself to pursue things that you actually do have control over. Your stress adds nothing. The weather is terrible? That's too bad. But instead of complaining and stressing about it, turn your mind to those aspects of your world you have realistic control over. Do you need to buy a better raincoat?

Is the Method Applicable?

Every problem in life, no matter how big or small, can be classed in one of these three categories. For the Stoics, stressing about things that were outside your realm of influence was illogical and only disturbed your state of mind. Instead, use what mental energy you have to carefully consider what you can change for the better, and how.

Technique 5: Yoga

Stop! Yoga Time

We've considered a few techniques and methods of managing everyday stress. Let's now shift our attention to a more practical, day-to-day way to deal with stress - yoga.

It's not necessary to fork out money for a monthly yoga studio membership or buy suitably stretchy yoga pants to enjoy the benefits of this ancient and highly relaxing art. Yoga improves flexibility, boosts bodily awareness and enhances your feelings of wellbeing. And you can do it right now!

The Best Time to Start Is Now!

First, take a moment to find your breath. Take a few exaggerated breaths in and out, feeling the oxygen as it spreads to each and every corner of your lungs. Feel it entering into your nostrils; note its temperature; listen carefully to the almost imperceptible sound it makes as it does so.

Connect Your Mind and Body

Next, you're going to pretend you're not a stressed person sitting on a computer, but rather a tall and majestic oak tree with the wind in its leaves. Inhale deeply and bring as much air as possible into the very tops of your lungs. When you feel you can hold no more, take in one more breath, just in case. Stretch your hands up above you, remembering to loosen and relax the shoulders. Reach up as tall as you possibly can and then let the head slowly tilt backwards, stretching the front of your neck. Now, gradually move into a backbend where you lift up and back as far as possible, stretching and extending the spine. Hold for a few moments, then repeat (feels good, doesn't it?).

Balance Yourself Out

Everything in life is in balance, and you should be too. So for your next move, gently tip the chin forward towards the chest while you imagine the base of your spine pushing up towards the ceiling. Feel the stretch all down the back of your neck and maintain your deep, relaxed breathing as you do.

Concentrate on Your Body

Let's not forget about those shoulders! Next, push your chair back and away from the desk and perch on the edge. Lean forward, reach your arms straight out in front of you and touch the desk with your fingertips. Imagine yourself as flat and straight as possible, the line from the base of your spine to the tips of your fingers laying horizontally. You can drop the head a little as you stretch out those shoulders from a long day of hunching in front of a screen.

Activate With a Twist

Next, try a gentle twist. Sitting upright in your chair again, slowly rotate the entire torso to one side, looking back over your shoulder and holding the armrest of your chair. Don't merely twist your shoulders, but activate your entire core to twist. Breathe deeply and then repeat on the other side.

The Final Stretch

Lastly, stretch out the back of the legs and release the spine by standing up for a refreshing stretch. Drop forward to touch your feet to the ground (or as close as you can get!) and keep the spine relaxed. There's no need to brace or lock your knees, but do push for a stretch. Breathe deeply and then move a little more into the stretch before coming back up again.

If you like, now's the time to explain to any confused colleagues what on earth you're up to.

CHAPTER 8

Helpful Tips

Practical Ways to Support a Stressed Body and Mind

Hopefully, you've identified a few ways to enhance your personal resilience and techniques to manage the inevitable daily stress that life brings. But remember that even the most serene, well-balanced person will take strain if they're put in an environment that is simply not conducive to mental wellbeing

Practical Ideas

1. **Consider using technology to help with time management.** Install apps that cut down on distractions (for example those that prevent you from mindless surfing online during specified hours) or note-keeping and calendar apps to help you keep track of a busy schedule.
2. **It's standard advice but still good advice exercise**. Anything that raises the pulse and gets you sweating will raise endorphin levels – perhaps there's also something about mastery of

the physical self that makes mastery of the mental self seem easier.

3. **Ask for help.** Even if nothing comes of you sharing your troubles with a friend, merely expressing yourself will lighten the load and help you feel connected to and supported by others. Sharing your troubles also gives you some perspective since you realise you're actually not alone.
4. **Delegate**: look at your to-do list and eliminate one thing that doesn't really need to be there, or ask someone better qualified to do it instead. Ask yourself seriously how much of the stress you choose to carry is really necessary.
5. **Don't deliberately work against your body when it comes to stress – cut down on or eliminate caffeine entirely.** Caffeine is a stimulant and the feeling of increased energy it provides can easily push an already stressed body over the edge. A possibility is to wean yourself off a caffeine addiction by switching to tea or decaf coffee.
6. **Examine your boundaries**. Often, we stress on behalf of someone else in the guise of caring for them. Worrying about something that you logically have no control over is not an expression of concern for someone else and will only leave you feeling depleted. Reinforce boundaries that defend your free time and examine whether you routinely allow others to violate these boundaries.

7. **Consider drinking** calming chamomile, valerian tea, or dabble a little in aromatherapy to make your immediate surroundings more comfortable.
8. **Try your best to reduce the amount of time you have to commute to work, or find ways to make the trip less stressful**. Take the train and listen to audiobooks to make use of the time, or wake up earlier to cut 20 minutes off the morning rush.
9. **Let go of perfectionism.** Stressing about having things 100% right is usually just a question of control. Re-examine what is truly under your control, forgive mistakes you make and pour energy into moving forward instead.
10. **Make sure your bedroom is set up to allow for proper sleep.** Invest in blackout curtains, a good mattress and quality bedding so you can give yourself the best chances to recuperate after each day.
11. **Get into the habit of converting worry into action** – and discarding those worrisome thoughts that can't be converted to anything useful. Worry spends a lot of mental effort but isn't in itself an action, and might even prevent you from acting. If you routinely worry about your health, get a full check-up to put your mind at ease, or make positive, healthy changes to your lifestyle, for example.
12. **Wherever possible, cut out heavily refined foods and processed sugar from your diet**.

These spike insulin levels and can leave you feeling burnt out and irritable.

13. **As corny as it sounds, laughter really is the best medicine**. Go out to an open mic comedy night, play practical jokes on your work colleagues and laugh at yourself when you make a mistake. Being able to see the absurd side of life is a true mark of a resilient person.

CHAPTER 9

When to See a Professional 1

Trauma and PTSD

No discussion about stress, worry and anxiety would be complete without a consideration of PTSD, or Post Traumatic Stress Disorder, as well as trauma. These are serious issues that will not simply disappear. They require your attention and professional help. What Is PTSD?

According to the Diagnostic and Statistical Manual, or the DSM, symptoms from three separate categories need to be present for a mental health professional to diagnose post-traumatic stress. A PTSD response can occur after any event that a person perceives to be life threatening, or else witnessing a life threatening situation occurring for someone else.

Your Perception Counts the Most

Importantly, the situation doesn't need to actually be life threatening – only perceived that way. What's more, the trauma needs to be understood at the time to be out of the person's control and unescapable. Vicarious trauma can occur when this intense feeling of being very close to death is experienced on someone else's behalf. Violent crimes, rape, war experiences, natural disasters and accidents can all fit this bill, but many people develop PTSD symptoms from merely the threat of these occurring.

Re-Experiencing Symptoms

When a human being's life is threatened, the entire organism becomes hyper-alert, ready to mobilise any resources needed to "fight or flight." It's theorised that this heightened state is what sharpens the memory for traumatic events, causing people to feel like details are painfully burnt or etched into the memory with more intensity than other memories.

Re-experiencing symptoms include flashbacks, intrusive nightmares or being unable to stop thoughts and memories of the event rushing into awareness. The mind may feel like it's "replaying" all the stressful parts of a horrible movie, perhaps in an attempt to make sense of what were incredibly upsetting stimuli.

Hypervigilance Symptoms

Stressful events can flood the body with adrenaline and cortisol, and cause ripple effects throughout the entire organism. The hypothalamus, pituitary gland and adrenal glands are in constant, delicate balance with each other and trauma can throw this out of whack.

What Is the Result of Hypervigilance?

It can include symptoms like insomnia, being unable to focus on what's at hand, jumpiness and a heightened startle response. Family members of those who suffer from PTSD know about this last phenomenon all too well: they'll approach their loved one from behind or surprise them in some way and their loved one may scream, jump or even lash out violently. It's as though the body's set point for panic has become disturbed, and the mind is constantly on the lookout for more potential trauma.

Avoidance Symptoms

The final cluster of symptoms, that may lead to a PTSD diagnosis, includes efforts to avoid everything that reminds the person of the original trauma. This could mean deliberately avoiding the street where a car accident occurred, ending conversations that might lead to discussion of the trauma, or even "forgetting" about information related to the event.

The human mind has a remarkable ability to learn and adapt to its environment, and wanting to prevent further trauma is understandable. Some PTSD sufferers may find themselves developing mild phobias around certain words, images or places due to the trauma they associate with them.

Could You Have PTSD?

Only a qualified professional can make a diagnosis. Lay people may be tempted to think that a particular event doesn't count as traumatic enough, or otherwise expect that a person should be more traumatised given a certain event. The truth is, we all respond differently to stress, and whether PTSD develops or not has to do with the intensity of the event, but also the person's appraisal of the situation.

A child, for example, may more readily feel out of control and threatened in a situation than an adult. Some researchers have found that in some cases, traumas like natural disasters are not as damaging psychologically as you would expect, probably because many people share the same experience and this feeling of bonding helps to moderate the feeling of helplessness that can trigger PTSD.

When to Seek a Professional?

If you or someone you know has experienced a traumatic event or is otherwise experiencing some of these symptoms, consult a professional. This is especially true if symptoms are getting in the way of work or relationships.

Treatment

Thankfully, treatment for PTSD is comprehensive and often has excellent outcomes. A psychiatrist or psychologist may prescribe anti-anxiety medication or suggest natural relaxant to bring about some calm. When combined with therapy, this can be extremely effective.

Therapeutic Practices

Therapeutic intervention can involve talking through the trauma to make sense of the event, as well as to learn coping techniques, share experiences and get relief that the problem is not unusual. The therapist may also gently suggest desensitising the person to stimuli they are avoiding, such as asking them to gradually become more comfortable getting back on horseback after a traumatic riding accident, for example.

Lastly, a therapist may also suggest ways to maintain a support network, provide information about the disorder and suggest mindfulness techniques or even prayer as a way to moderate the stress response and find some meaning in the trauma.

CHAPTER 10

When to See a Professional 2

Generalised **Anxiety**, **OCD**, and **Phobias**
In the same cases, seeking out a professional mental health specialist may be necessary. This is nothing negative. In fact, the right specialist can help you achieve a much calmer state of mind and feel a lot happier.

Sometimes, worry, stress and anxiety go beyond our everyday ability to cope. If the techniques covered in this course don't help, if your symptoms are becoming worse or your doctor recommends it, you may need to seek more comprehensive treatment and consider medication or therapy.

When Is Professional Help Most Useful?

Not sure if you should seek professional help? The following are some red flags:

- You have a phobia or fear or something specific that is interfering with your everyday life.
- Your work and home life are beginning to suffer because of your anxiety.
- You find yourself having intrusive thoughts or obsessively checking, washing your hands or doing little rituals that you can't seem to stop engaging in.

- You feel incredibly depressed; your anxiety makes you want to harm yourself or others.
- Your anxiety is causing you to neglect your hygiene, health, or safety.
- You're dealing with your anxiety and worry by abusing substances like alcohol.

Where to Look for Help?
If you're concerned, chat to your GP, a trusted friend or book an appointment with a mental health professional. You could also enquire about help lines or support groups in your area.

On the Road to a Calmer Lifestyle

I'm almost done with my guide - you have learnt heaps and are now hopefully able to apply most, if not all, to your own life. However, to achieve true improvement and success, you need to keep going, even when you finish reading this book.

Hopefully, you've had the opportunity to take a deeper look at how, when and why you worry – and what you can do today to start taking charge of your own wellness.

What Did We Do During This guide?
In this book, we've tried first to understand fear, anxiety and worry, and then find ways to cope and be more resilient in the face of everyday stress.

We've looked at ways to be more mindful, ways to take control of worrying thoughts, and practical techniques to stay strong not only in our minds, but also in our bodies. Lastly, we took a look at what to do when worry becomes more serious, briefly considering more troubling forms our worry can take.

Use Your Journal as a Reference Point

As we finish this guide, it might be useful to go back through the journal you started in the very beginning. Compare your state of mind at the start to your state of mind now. Has anything changed?

What is Next?

Consider what techniques and exercises you found the most helpful. Also think about the areas where you are still hoping to improve, and think about ways you might approach that. Be patient with yourself – you may still have some stressful and worry-heavy days, but try to remind yourself of all the skills you've learnt and stop, take a breath, relax. A calm, happy lifestyle is built slowly, one moment at a time.

The End of the guide Is Not the End of Your Journey

As the course comes to its end, I encourage you to keep improving and working on your calmer, happier life. To give you a boost - can you think of one way you'd like to continue onwards, now that the course is finished? What single thing can you do once you're done reading here that will improve your state of mind, right now?

Let's do it then!

www.ingramcontent.com/pod-product-compliance
Lightning Source LLC
LaVergne TN
LVHW050335160826
845677LV00014B/3621

* 9 7 9 8 3 5 2 7 6 6 2 6 2 *